———————

Community Helpers

Mechanics

by Cari Meister

Bullfrog Books

Ideas for Parents and Teachers

Bullfrog Books let children practice reading informational text at the earliest reading levels. Repetition, familiar words, and photo labels support early readers.

Before Reading

- Discuss the cover photo. What does it tell them?

- Look at the picture glossary together. Read and discuss the words.

Read the Book

- "Walk" through the book and look at the photos. Let the child ask questions. Point out the photo labels.

- Read the book to the child, or have him or her read independently.

After Reading

- Prompt the child to think more. Ask: Do you know anyone who is a mechanic? What other kinds of machines might a mechanic fix?

Bullfrog Books are published by Jump!
5357 Penn Avenue South
Minneapolis, MN 55419
www.jumplibrary.com

Library of Congress Cataloging-in-Publication Data
Meister, Cari.
  Mechanics / by Cari Meister.
    pages cm.—(Community helpers)
  Includes bibliographical references and index.
  Summary: "This photo-illustrated book for early readers explains the different kinds of mechanics and the machines that they fix, including cars, missiles, and ships"—Provided by publisher.
  ISBN 978-1-62031-093-9 (hardcover)
  ISBN 978-1-62496-161-8 (ebook)
  ISBN 978-1-62031-137-0 (paperback)
  1. Automobile mechanics—Juvenile literature. 2. Automobiles—Maintenance and repair—Juvenile literature. I. Title.
  TL152.M385 2015
  620.1023—dc23
                                        2013042372

Editor: Wendy Dieker
Series Designer: Ellen Huber
Book Designer: Lindaanne Donohoe
Photo Researcher: Kurtis Kinneman

Photo Credits: All photos by Shutterstock except Alamy, 14, 18-19; iStock 8-9, 16-17; Superstock 12-13

Printed in the United States of America at Corporate Graphics, North Mankato, Minnesota.
6-2014
10 9 8 7 6 5 4 3 2 1

Table of Contents

At Work in the Shop

Trey wants to be a mechanic.

What do they do?

They fix broken things.

Nick fixes cars.
He has a wrench.
It takes off bolts.
Now he can see
what is wrong.

wrench and bolt

Abe fixes jets.

earmuffs

It is loud.

He wears earmuffs.

Rob works at a power plant.

He checks the machines.

He fixes them.

Jo is in the army.
She checks missiles.

14

She makes sure they work.

missile

Kyle works on a ship.

Oh no! A part is broken.

He helps fix it.

Joel works on
tractors.

He takes off
an old tire.

He puts on
a new one.

tire

Mechanics do good work!

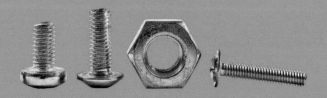

At the Shop

lift
A machine that lifts and holds heavy machines or parts so that mechanics can work on them.

tool chest
A set of drawers to hold and organize tools.

Picture Glossary

bolt
A metal pin that holds things together.

power plant
A factory where electricity or other power is made.

missile
An exploding rocket or bomb.

wrench
A tool that tightens and loosens nuts and bolts.

23

Index

To Learn More

Learning more is as easy as 1, 2, 3.

1) Go to www.factsurfer.com

2) Enter "mechanics" into the search box.

3) Click the "Surf" button to see a list of websites.

With factsurfer.com, finding more information is just a click away.